02-3741

A New True Book

HORSES

By Elsa Posell

This "true book" was prepared
under the direction of
Illa Podendorf,
formerly with the Laboratory School,
University of Chicago

CHILDRENS PRESS, CHICAGO

Morgan gelding

PHOTO CREDITS

Bobbie Lieberman, Equus—2, 4 (2 photos), 6, 8 (2 photos), 13, 17, 27 (bottom), 28, 33 (2 photos), 37, 38, 41 (2 photos), 42 (right), 45 (top)

Carl Miller, Equus—11

Barry Thompson, Equus—14

Richard Wahl—19

James P. Rowan—21

Connecticut Department of Economic Development—23 (above)

Wyoming Travel Commission—23 (below)

Chicago Historical Society—24

American Saddlebred Horse Association, Inc.— Cover, 27 (top), 39

United States Department of Agriculture—29

Chicago Police Department—30

Welsh Pony Society of America—35

Department of Tourist Development, State of Tennessee—42 (left)

Anheuser-Busch, Inc—45 (left)

Idaho Division of Tourism and Industrial Development—45

Library of Congress Cataloging in Publication Data

Posell, Elsa Z.
  Horses.

  (A New true book)
  Previously published as: The true book of horses. 1961.
  Summary: Briefly traces the growth and training of a foal, weanling, and yearling, discusses the history and uses of horses in America, and describes various kinds of horses.
  1. Horses—Juvenile literature. [1. Horses] I. Title.
SF302.P67   1981   636.1   81-7741
ISBN 0-516-01623-7   AACR2

TABLE OF CONTENTS

Foal with mother

Two-hour-old foal rolls in the grass

THE FOAL

A baby horse is called a foal. A foal is born with a coat of curly hair. This coat becomes straight as the foal grows up.

Unlike some baby animals, a foal can see when it is born. It can stand up, too.

Arabian foal drinking its mother's milk.

A foal stays with its mother. It drinks her warm milk. For the next few months the foal eats, sleeps, and grows.

When a foal is only a few hours old, its owner talks to it softly. The foal smells its owner's hand. The foal soon learns not to be afraid of people.

Weanlings run and play in the pasture.

THE WEANLING

A foal is taken from its mother when it is four or five months old. It is then called a weanling. It learns to live without its mother. It eats grass, hay, and grain. It gallops, runs, and plays.

If the weanling is a male, it is called a colt. If it is a female, it is a filly.

The mother horse is a mare. The father is called a stallion.

Most weanlings have
some lessons every day.
They learn to be led with
a halter of soft, flat rope.
At first this seems strange
to the weanlings.

People who train weanlings must be gentle. They talk to them. They groom them with soft brushes and pick up their feet. The young horses get used to having their feet handled. Later they can be shoed without becoming afraid.

Yearling thoroughbred colt resting in the sun.

THE YEARLING

In their second year, young horses are called yearlings. They are old enough to learn to carry people on their backs.

The yearling first gets used to the feel of a pad on his back. After that, a saddle is strapped to his back. Before long, a rider can climb into the saddle and be carried by the yearling.

Some horses are ready to go to work by the time they reach two years old.

A horse is full-grown in five to seven years.

Some horses live for thirty years. But most horses live for fifteen or twenty years.

Mare with her foal

A mare, or mother horse,
may have her first foal
when she is four years old.

HORSES HELPED OUR COUNTRY GROW

At one time there were no horses in America.

Spanish explorers on horseback were a strange and wonderful sight to Indians.

Soon, one way or another, the Indians got some of these horses for themselves.

Indians of the plains
found horses a help in
following the herds of
buffalo.

As settlers came to live in America, more horses were brought into the country.

A horse could carry a man through the places where there were no roads. A man often owed his life to his horse.

Farm horses at Billy Creek Village.

Horses were helpful in many ways. They pulled heavy logs and stones to build cabins. They helped clear the land and plow the fields.

Horses pulled covered wagons for families moving west. They pulled stagecoaches. As towns and cities grew, lively horses pulled pretty carriages in which people rode around the town.

Horse-drawn sleigh

Covered wagons on the trail in Wyoming

1903 photograph of a horse-drawn streetcar.

At one time, horses pulled streetcars. Other well-trained horses pulled the fire engines.

Horses pulled wagons full of food and other things.

For many years, soldiers used horses to carry them and to haul their wagons.

Small, fast horses carried the mail from Missouri to California. This was the Pony Express, before the railroad crossed the country. Riders rode at top speed and changed horses every 10 or 12 miles.

HORSES TODAY

Today we have planes, trains, cars, and machines. But people still have and use many horses.

People love horses and ride them for pleasure.

Some farmers still have horses that work for them.

Beautiful trained horses prance in the circus.

Many horses learn to be very gentle with young riders.
Some horses are trained to be jumpers.

A polo pony is really a small horse. He is trained to turn quickly and to follow the ball.

Beautiful Thoroughbred horses are raised and trained as race horses.

Race horse

What would a ranch be without horses? Ranch horses can do many things. They carry cowboys through rough country to look for lost cattle. They work as hard as a rider who is roping and branding calves.

A bucking bronco in a rodeo may be a horse that could not be tamed.

In many cities, the police ride horses. Their horses must be strong, smart, and gentle.

Police horses in Chicago

The horses are trained with their masters in police stables. They learn to work in noise and heavy traffic. They learn to step aside to let cars pass. They can move in crowds without hurting anyone.

A police horse has only one master who loves it and gives it the best of care.

Sometimes the hoofs of a police horse are packed with tar and cloth. This helps protect its feet from the hard, hot, summer pavements.

A horse's hoofs are
made of horn.
Horn is hard.
Before blacksmiths put
shoes on the horse's
hoofs, they make sure
the hoofs are clean.
They file the hoof
so it is smooth.
Then they carefully tap
in special nails to hold
the shoe in place.

PONIES

The width of a man's hand is about 4 inches. When we say a horse is 15 hands high, it is 15 times 4 inches high.

A pony is a small horse, less than 14 hands high.

A Shetland pony is sometimes only 8 hands high.

Welsh Pony

A Welsh pony is usually about 12 to 14 hands high.

A HORSE NEEDS CARE

A horse needs good care and kindness to be healthy and useful.

It needs good food, water, and exercise. A horse should cool off after exercise before it has a drink.

A horse's coat needs a good rubdown. It should be combed from head to tail with a rubber comb. Its feet and legs should be washed with a sponge when they are dirty.

Four-and-one-half-month-old horse

A pony does not eat
much. But a grown
working horse may eat all
of this in one day:
●Seven pounds of corn
and oats
●Eight to twelve pounds

of timothy, alfalfa or clover hay

• A salt lick

As a snack, an apple, a carrot, or turnips are a treat.

All horses like to nibble the fresh pasture grass.

Saddlebred horses in pasture

ALL KIND OF HORSES

All horses are alike in many ways. But it is fun to see how different they are, too.

An Arabian is small, smart, beautiful, and strong. It is often ridden as a show horse.

Above: A seven-year old Thoroughbred named Christopher

Right: An Arabian mare with her two-hour-old foal.

Thoroughbred horses first came from England. Many of them are now raised for racing and jumping.

The American Saddle horse is bigger than the Arabian.

The Morgan is a true American horse.

The Tennessee walking horse is related to the Morgan.

Right: Palomino Quarter Horse
Below: Tennessee Walking Horse

The Standard Bred horse is seen in trotting races.

A quarter horse got its name from its speed in quarter-mile races.

Horses that do heavy work are called draft horses. One of the largest of these is the Belgian.

The Cleveland Bay is smaller and good for work on a farm.

The Clydesdale looks feather-footed.

The Percheron's back is broad enough to hold a circus dancer.

The Shire horse comes from England.

Some horses are named for their color or markings, not their breed.

Horses are fine, beautiful animals that give us help and pleasure.

Clydesdale

Percheron-type mare

Appaloosa Horse

WORDS YOU SHOULD KNOW

alfalfa(al • FAL • fa) — a plant that is grown for food for animals

Appaloosa(ap • uh • LOO • sah) — a type of horse having different colors on its coat

Arabian(ah • RAY • be • in) — a kind of horse which is known for being a fast runner

Belgian horse(BEL • jin HORSE) — a large, strong horse used to do heavy work

brand — a mark burned into the skin of animals to show who owns them

breed — a certain kind of animal

bucking bronco(BUK • ing BRAHN • koh) — a horse that jumps forward and upward, twists and turns

calf(KAF) — young cattle

carriage(KAIR • ij) — a cart for people usually pulled by horses

clover(KLOH • ver) — a small green plant grown for food for animals

Clydesdale(KLYDS • dayl) — a large, strong horse used to do heavy work

coat(KOHT) — the hair or fur of an animal

colt(KOHLT) — a young male horse

explorer(eks • PLOHR • er) — a person who travels in unknown places

filly(FIL • ee) — a young female horse

foal(FOHL) — a young horse

halter — a set of ropes put around a horse's head so it can be led or tied

mare(MAIR) — a female horse

master — a person who owns an animal

Morgan(MOR • gun) — a light horse used for riding

nibble(NIB • il) — to take small, quick bites

palomino(pal • oh • ME • noh) — a horse used in riding with a golden coat

pasture(PAS • cher) — land covered with grass or other plants

pavement(PAYV • ment) — a hard covering used on streets and roads

Percheron(PER • chuh • ron) — a strong horse with a gray or black coat used to do heavy work

pinto — a horse with spots or other markings

plains(PLAYNS) — a large, flat piece of land with no trees

plow — a farm tool used to break up the soil

polo pony — a horse which is ridden to play the game polo

prance(PRANTS) — to spring on two back legs and move forward

quarter horse(KWOR • ter horss) — a horse used in racing

saddle(SAD • uhl) — a seat placed on the back of a horse for a rider

settler(SET • ler) — a person who moves to a new region to live

Shetland pony — a small strong horse

Shire horse(SHY • er hors) — a large, strong horse with a brown coat used to do heavy work

shod — to put horseshoes on a horse

stable(STAY • bul) — a building where horses are kept

stagecoach(STAYJ • kohch) — a covered wagon with four wheels which was pulled by horses

stallion(STAL • yun) — a male horse

Thoroughbred(THIR • uh • bred) — a pure breed

Timothy hay(TIM • uh • thee HAY) — a type of tough grass which is used as animal food

weanling(WEEN • ling) — a horse that no longer drinks its mother's milk

Welsh pony — small, strong horse

width — the distance of something from one side to the other

yearling — a horse in its second year

INDEX

About the Author

Elsa Posell received her M.S. in Library Science from Western Reserve University. She has been a librarian in the Cleveland Heights Public Schools, and is currently devoting over half her time to work with children in the Cleveland area and other Ohio counties in language arts, story telling, and creative writing. As a story teller and lecturer Mrs. Posell has worked in schools in Korea, Japan, Hong Kong, and China. One of her books, This is an Orchestra, *is published in Japanese. Mrs. Posell is also the author of* American Composers, Russian Music and Musicians, Russian Authors, *and* Beginning Book of Knowledge of Seashells.

A New True Book

TIME

By Feenie Ziner and Elizabeth Thompson

*This "true book" was prepared
under the direction of
Illa Podendorf,
formerly with the Laboratory School,
University of Chicago*

CHILDRENS PRESS ™

CHICAGO

PHOTO CREDITS

Picture Group—John Sheckler—Cover,
Philip Jon Bailey—2, 40

Len Meents—8

Reinhard Brucker—4, 22, 43 (bottom)

Candee & Associates—6, 26 (right), 30, 32
(right), 36, 38 (bottom), 44

Smithsonian Institution—10 (2 photos), 11,
13, 14, 19, 20

Courtesy of The Oriental Institute—The
University of Chicago—17

Courtesy of The Time Museum, Rockford,
Illinois—24, 26 (left), 27, 35, 38 (top),
43 (top right).

Margarit Fiddle—28, 32 (left)

Al Rutzen—43 (top left)

COVER—City Hall Clock, New Bedford,
Massachusetts

Library of Congress Cataloging in Publication Data

Ziner, Feenie.
  Time.

  (A New true book)
  Rev. ed. of: The true book of time. 1956.
  Summary: Presents various methods of telling
time by using such instruments as the shadow
stick, sundial, candle clock, rope clock, water
clock, hourglass, and the modern clock.
    1. Time—Juvenile literature. [1. Time.
2. Clocks and watches—History] I. Thompson,
Elizabeth Signe. II. Title.
QB209.5.Z56   1982   529'.7   81-18080
ISBN 0-516-01651-2   AACR2

TABLE OF CONTENTS

Sunset

DAY AND NIGHT

How do you know what time it is?

You can tell something about time by looking at the sun.

It is morning at sunrise.

It is noon when the sun is highest in the sky.

It is evening when the sun sets.

At night the moon shines on Earth. At the same time the sun is shining on the other side of the Earth.

When the sun shines on the other side of our planet Earth, it is night for us.

But you cannot count hours just by looking at the sun.

SHADOW STICKS

A shadow stick can help us count the hours.

A shadow stick points straight up. The stones around the stick mark the hours.

A shadow stick is like a clock.

As the Earth turns, the
sun makes the shadow of
the stick fall on the stones.

The shadow moves from one stone to the next in one hour.

Can you tell time on a cloudy day with a shadow stick?

No.

Can you tell time at night with a shadow stick?

No.

Two examples of American sundials

Although this
sundial has a
different shape,
it works just
like the sundials
shown on page 10.

SUNDIALS

A sundial is like a
shadow stick. It can only
tell time when the sun is
shining.

CANDLE CLOCKS

There is a way to tell time that works both night and day.

It works when it is sunny or cloudy.

It is a candle clock.

A candle clock is painted with bands of color. It takes an hour for each band to burn.

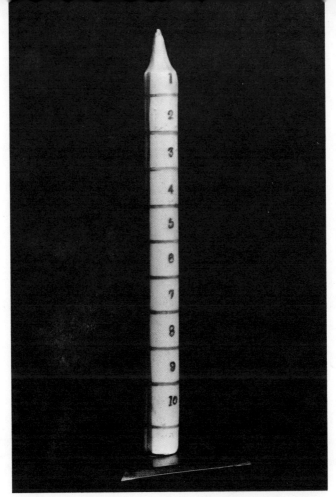

Model of a
King Alfred
candle clock

If you light a candle clock at 8 o'clock and burn 2 bands what time will it be?

Ten o'clock.

14   Example of a time rope, part of the
Smithsonian Institution's collection

ROPE CLOCKS

People can count hours by burning ropes. They tie knots in the rope to mark the hours.

People in Korea once used rope clocks.

It takes one hour for the rope to burn from one knot to the next.

Candle clocks and rope clocks do not need the sun.

Can the candle clock or the rope clock be used over again?

No.

Ancient Egyptian water clock made about 2200 years ago

WATER CLOCKS

Water clocks were used long, long ago.

The first water clock measured the water leaking out of a big pot.

Different water lines were marked on the pot—one for each hour. People could tell time by looking at the line and the water left in the pot.

Water clocks did not need the sun. They could work at night. They could be used over and over again.

HOURGLASS

Another way of telling
time is with an hourglass.
It has an unusual shape.
Sand falls from the top
to the bottom.
This takes one hour.

Then the glass is turned upside down.

An hourglass and a water clock can be used again and again.

HOW TO TELL TIME

Do you know how to tell time?

Or do you ask someone else, "What time is it?"

The short hand points to 3. It is 3 o'clock.

People look at the clock to find out what time it is.

How does the clock tell them the time?

The short hand points to the hours.

It takes an hour for the short hand to move from one number to the next.

There are 24 hours in a day. A day lasts from midnight to midnight. This is how much time it takes the Earth to turn around once.

The Earth turns once every 24 hours.

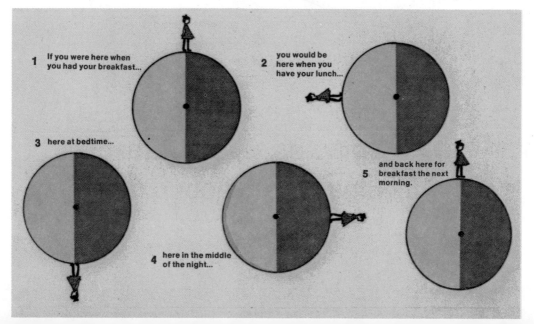

1 If you were here when you had your breakfast...

2 you would be here when you have your lunch...

3 here at bedtime...

4 here in the middle of the night...

5 and back here for breakfast the next morning.

The long hand points to
the minutes. There are 60
minutes in an hour.

The long hand goes all around the clock once every hour. It tells how many minutes after the hour it is.

It takes 5 minutes for the long hand to move from one number to the next.

Most clocks count minutes by fives.

Some clocks count seconds, too. There are 60 seconds in a minute.

Above: Clock using Arabic numerals
Left: Clock using Roman numerals

Most clocks have numbers from 1 to 12. But some clocks have special numbers called Roman numerals.

Can you tell time on this kind of clock?

The chart tells you what the Roman numerals mean. Now can you tell what time it is? If you said 6 o'clock, you are correct.

Roman numeral		Arabic numeral
I	equals	1
II	=	2
III	=	3
IV	=	4
V	=	5
VI	=	6
VII	=	7
VIII	=	8
IX	=	9
X	=	10
XI	=	11
XII	=	12

You know that when the clock reads 12 o'clock during the day it is noontime. Noon is the middle of the day. Most people eat around noontime.

At night when the short hand points to 12 it is midnight. This is the middle of the night. Most people are asleep at midnight.

On most clocks, the short hand goes around two times in 24 hours.

A 24-hour clock on display at the Museum of Science and
Industry in Chicago, Illinois

24-HOUR CLOCKS

Some clocks are 24-hour clocks. Each hour of the day has its own number.

On this clock at noon the hour hand would point to 12. When the hour hand points to 00 it would be midnight. Midnight is hour number 24.

Above: 12-hour clock
Right: 24-hour clock

Look at these two
clocks. One is a 12-hour
clock. The other is a 24-
hour clock.

The 12 hour clock reads 2 o'clock and the sun is shining. At 2 o'clock what number would the hour hand point to on the 24-hour clock? Remember each hour has its own number.

Did you say 14? If you were telling time on a 24-hour clock, the hour hand would be pointing to 14.

The army uses the 24-hour clock. With this clock there is no mistake about night and day because each hour has its own number.

Early digital clock made by Gillett and Craydon about 1880

DIGITAL CLOCKS

Today we have clocks that do not have hands. They are called digital clocks. Do you know how to tell time on this kind of clock?

Look at this clock. The
first number shown tells
you the hour.

It is 3 o'clock.

The number after the
colon tells you the
minutes. It is 12 minutes
after the hour.

Plato digital clock made by E.L. Fitch, New York, in 1902. This was one of the four basic models made by the Ansonia Clock Company.

A modern digital clock

Can you tell what time it
is on the two clocks
shown on page 38?

The top clock tells you it
is 4 o'clock. On the other
clock the time is 2:56. It
is 56 minutes after 2 o'clock.
In four more minutes
it will be 3 o'clock.
Remember there are 60
minutes in an hour.

Sometimes it is hard to tell the hour hand from the minute hand.
But if you look closely you can see a difference. This clock
tells you it's 21 minutes after twelve.

THINGS TO REMEMBER

The short hand points to the hours.

It takes one hour for the short hand to move from one number to the next.

There are 24 hours in a day.

The long hand points to the minutes in an hour. There are 5 minutes between each number. The long hand tells how many minutes after the hour it is.

Clocks are made
in all sizes and
shapes.

Big Ben is a famous clock in London, England.

The long hand moves all around the clock while the short hand is going from one number to the next.

There are 60 seconds in one minute.

Some clocks are 24-hour clocks. Each hour has its own number.

WORDS YOU SHOULD KNOW

Arabic numerals(AIR • ih • bik NOOM • er • ilz) —The numbers 1, 2, 3, 4, 5, 6, 7, 8, 9, and 0

candle clock(KAN • dil CLAHK) —a candle painted with bands of color that take one hour each to burn

digital clock(DIJ • ih • til CLAHK) —a clock that tells time in number units

hour(OUR) —a unit of time that is equal to sixty minutes

hourglass(OUR • glass) —an instrument used to measure time

minute(MIN • it) —a unit of time equal to sixty seconds

noon —middle of the day; twelve o'clock in the daytime

queer(KWEER) —unusual; odd; strange

Roman numerals(ROH • min NOOM • er • ilz) —letters used by ancient Romans to stand for numbers.
For example I=1, V=5, X=10,
L=50, C=100, D=500
M=1000

shadow stick(SHAD • oh STIK) —an instrument used to measure time by the sun

sundial(SUN • dyle) —an instrument used to tell time by the sun

INDEX

About the Authors

Feenie Ziner and Elizabeth Thompson have years of experience working with children both in and out of the classroom. Their background prompted them to write this fascinating look at the different devices people have used to measure time.